Samuel

By Bobbi Katz

Illustrated by Pat Reynolds

HOUGHTON MIFFLIN COMPANY

BOSTON

ATLANTA   DALLAS   GENEVA, ILLINOIS   PALO ALTO   PRINCETON

I found this salamander
near the pond in the woods.
Samuel, I called him—
Samuel, Samuel.

Right away I loved him.
He loved me too, I think.
Samuel, I called him—
Samuel, Samuel.

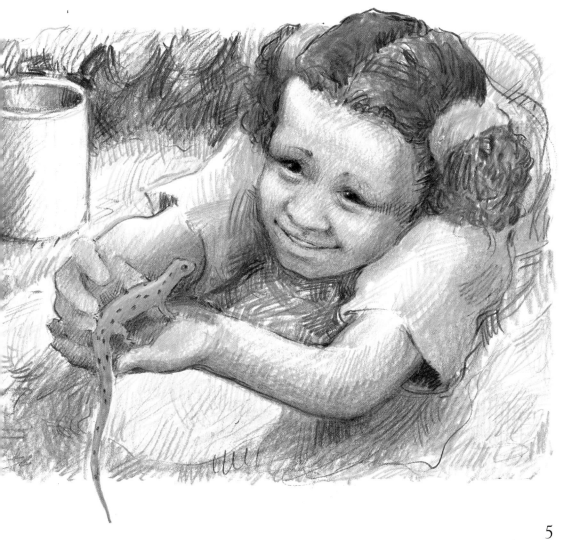

I took him home in a coffee can,
and at night he slept in my bed.

In the morning I took him to school.

He died very quietly during spelling.

Sometimes I think I should have left him near the pond in the woods.

Samuel, I called
him—
Samuel, Samuel.